GOD COULD BE A TEEN...
NO ONE UNDERSTANDS HIM EITHER

God Could Be a Teen…
No One Understands Him, Either

The Truth and Freedom
of Catholic Morality

JAMES PENRICE

ALBA·HOUSE   N E W · Y O R K

SOCIETY OF ST. PAUL, 2187 VICTORY BLVD., STATEN ISLAND, NEW YORK 10314

ST PAULS

Library of Congress Cataloging-in-Publication Data

Penrice, James, 1961-
    God could be a teen — no one understands him either: the truth
and freedom of Catholic morality / James Penrice.
        p.   cm.
    Includes bibliographical references.
    ISBN 0-8189-0777-0
    1. Christian ethics — Catholic authors. 2. Sexual ethics for
teenagers. 3. Social ethics. I. Title.
    BJ1249.P366   1997
    241'.042 — dc21   96-40936
                                                CIP

Produced and designed in the United States of America by the
Fathers and Brothers of the Society of St. Paul,
2187 Victory Boulevard, Staten Island, New York 10314,
as part of their communications apostolate.

ISBN: 0-8189-0777-0

Printing Information:

Current Printing - first digit   1 2 3 4 5 6 7 8 9 10

Year of Current Printing - first year shown

1997   1998   1999   2000   2001   2002   2003

In gratitude to
Pope John Paul II,
for boldly proclaiming
The Splendor of Truth
and
The Gospel of Life

Table of Contents

Christianity is not that mass
of restrictions which the unbeliever
imagines; it is peace, joy, life and love which,
like the unseen throbbing of nature in
early spring, is ever being renewed.

Pope John XXIII

GOD COULD BE A TEEN…
NO ONE UNDERSTANDS HIM EITHER

PART ONE:

I Know the Rules; I Need the Truth

You want to be loved, but not everybody loves you. There are people you want to have a relationship with who don't love you back — and it hurts. People misunderstand you. You're a very complicated person, but others see only what's on the outside, and they jump to conclusions about you that aren't true. People tell false stories about you. You have ideas which you know are good, but others make fun of them as being weird. You get blamed for problems that aren't your fault. You know that if people would only make the effort to get to know you, if they gave you a chance to reveal who you really are, they would understand you better and love you. But you're frustrated that this doesn't always happen.

Don't let it get you down, God — it happens to me, too.

* * *

If only we could recognize how much we have in common with God.

But how could any human being possibly have anything in common with God? After all, we're "only human." We're not God; we're far from him. God is eternal, almighty, perfect in every way. We're mortal, sinful, imperfect, and we make many mistakes. We see such a huge difference between God and ourselves that we can't understand what we could possibly have in common with him. So we persist in our "humanness," excusing all of our behavior on the grounds that we're "only human," and that it is only natural to give into our weaknesses and to sin.

Because of this difference we see between God and ourselves, many of the Church's teachings on morality seem unreasonable — opposed to our basic human nature and therefore too demanding. The Church itself, after all, teaches that we're all born with original sin, and so we're all sinners. Wouldn't sinning, then, be only natural — "only human"? From that perspective the Church's moral teachings would seem unnatural and disordered.

Sex only in marriage? Why? Isn't it only natural for two people who are attracted to each other and are in love to have sex? (Or, if there is no one to have sex with, to give oneself an outlet for sexual desires?) What's more natural than to look after our own interests, even if it sometimes means having to lie or steal — especially if nobody gets hurt? What's more natural than to vent our anger at others, or to talk about or laugh at people when we find them different? What's more natural than to want pleasures, be they from material possessions, alcohol, drugs, sex, or whatever else brings us comfort? What's so wrong with that?

Besides, isn't it a denial of our freedom when someone tells us which behaviors are right and which are wrong? Doesn't being human mean being free to choose what's best for us and for our loved ones? God made us free to make our own choices. Aren't the Church's rules then an offense against that God-given freedom?

It would seem from this point of view that anyone who would try to deny our freedom and stop us from doing what simply comes naturally must be unreasonable and out of touch with what it means to be human. It would seem that the Church doesn't know what it's talking about when it establishes rules for living. Only someone who fully understands the human condition should be qualified to make rules for it. To many people the Church seems to be too preoccupied with God to understand what it means to be human.

It's true that as human beings we all sin. We're weak and liable to temptation and to sin; all of us do bad things and commit evils of one sort or another. All of us. But does that necessarily mean that sin and evil are a normal part of our human nature? When we look at the results which sin and evil produce in our lives, it becomes questionable just how natural these things really are to humanity. Thomas Merton, a Catholic priest who wrote many books on the spiritual life, made this interesting observation about sin, evil and human nature:

> Note of course that the doctrine of original sin, properly understood, is optimistic. It does not teach that man is by nature evil, but that evil in him is unnatural, a disorder, a sin. If evil, lying and hatred were natural to man, all men would be perfectly at home, perfectly happy in evil. Perhaps a few seem to find contentment in an unnatural state of falsity, hatred and greed. They are not happy. Or if they are, they are unnatural.

Merton's point is simple, but very important. If evil were a normal part of human nature, then all people would be happy living in evil. But we're not — evil brings pain and misery, loneliness and unhappiness. The reason evil causes misery is because it is not part of our nature; it is contrary to it. It is not human to give into the temptation of evil; it actually makes us less than human. Evil is something outside of us that we are drawn to because it is deceptively attractive and is easy to do. But since it is not in our nature, once we have participated in evil we feel pain, unhappiness, and above all a sense of emptiness because we aren't reaching our full potential as human beings.

So what does it really mean to be human? It means to be created in the image and likeness of God!

> So God created humankind in his image, in the image of God he created them; male and female he created them. *Genesis 1:27*

To be human does not mean to be far removed from God, or evil and sinful, but to be in God's own image and likeness! To be human means to have a lot in common with God, sharing his beautiful and awesome qualities. To be human means, like God, to be loving, forgiving, compassionate, creative. It means to be faithful, hopeful, just, strong, wise, temperate.

Once we recognize the image and likeness of God in ourselves and in the others he created, we need to rethink many of our old ideas about human nature, and what kind of behavior is really natural to us.

As people created in the image of a loving God, how natural is it to hate? To be selfish, unforgiving, or to lack compassion? To use other people for our pleasure? To destroy something God has created or to claim a right to his creative process?

As people created in the image of a faithful God, how natural is it to break our commitments and to abandon others, or to not make commitments at all?

As people created in the image of a hopeful God, how natural is it to give into despair and to surrender to the forces of evil?

As people created in the image of a just God, how natural is it to exploit others — either individuals or groups — denying them their dignity as human persons?

As people created in the image of a strong God, how natural is it to neglect the weak who need our help, or to be afraid to enter into relationships and to love?

As people created in the image of a wise God, how natural is it to live with ignorance or prejudice, with closed minds which make no effort to find the truth?

As people created in the image of a temperate God, how natural is it to give into our passions and to thus be controlled by them?

Many people see the Church's moral teachings as nothing more than a list of rules. But what it comes down to is this: the moral teachings of the Church are not rules; they're *truths* of how a fully human life is lived in the dignity with which God created every human person. Seeing Church teachings as rules rather than as truths only leads to a sense of emptiness, where goodness is sought outside the person rather than recognized within.

Rules are only followed out of a hope for reward or a fear of punishment. That's no way to live. Truth is recognized for what it is — the only way to *really* live. A fulfilled life cannot be found simply by following rules. The problem with rules is that they are easily broken. The truth is indestructible! The good news of Christianity is that no matter how many times we break those fragile rules, the truth which stands behind them can never be broken. It will always be there to return to, and it is that truth — not rules — that really fulfills our lives.

Pope John Paul II explains this difference between rules and truth very well in his encyclical *Veritatis Splendor (The Splendor of Truth)*. He cites the story of the rich young man who approaches Jesus and asks, "Teacher, what good must I do to have eternal life?" (Matthew 19:16). Pope John Paul II writes, "For the young man, the question is not so much about rules to be followed, but about the full meaning of life." When Jesus tells the young man to keep the commandments of God, the young man replies, "I have kept all these; what do I still lack?" (Matthew 19:20). In other words, the young man has followed all the rules but he still feels empty — he does not feel the full "reward" he expected and so his life still lacks something. That's because life is not simply about following rules. It is about entering into a full love relationship with Jesus Christ and letting his love seep into the depths of our being, filling our empty spaces and bringing us real fulfillment, real meaning, real peace.

That's the role Church teaching plays in our lives. It points us towards the fullest, deepest relationship we can have with God. It therefore points us to the fullest realization of our humanity, for all human beings were created by God in order to be in relationship with him. How deep our relationship becomes depends on how closely we live by the truth and let it into our hearts.

Jesus' response to the young man sounds disturbing: "If you wish to be perfect, go, sell your possessions and give the money to the poor, and you will have treasure in heaven; then come, follow me" (Matthew 19:21-22).

The possessions Jesus asks us to give up in order to follow him are the attachments we have to things which lead us away from our full humanity — our selfish desires, our cruel habits, our attraction to evil. He asks us to give these up so that we can be true to our human nature as good and loving people. Jesus is God become human, the fullest, most perfect expression of what humanity is. When Jesus dwells in us, we become closer to that fullest expression ourselves.

At first glance, many of the Church's teachings appear to restrict our freedom, urging us to do things we might not otherwise choose to do. Yet instead of limiting our freedom, the Church's teachings actually help us to become free. As Pope John Paul II further states in *Veritatis Splendor*, "Human freedom and God's law are not in opposition; on the contrary, they appeal one to the other." To understand this we have to learn what freedom really is.

Human beings by nature are good; that is what God made us to be. We are only free, therefore, when we can become what we were created to be. Anything which keeps us from reaching our full potential as human persons thus limits our freedom. It enslaves us, keeping us from reaching our destiny.

God's truth brings us the freedom to reach our full potential as people created in his loving image. Evil behavior enslaves us, traps us, keeps us from being who we really are. When we are acting in bad ways it is not really out of freedom, though we may think we are freely choosing our actions. Rather, it is because evil is interfering with our natural instinct for goodness, and is thus controlling us. We need to follow God's natural ways in order to be freed from the slavery of evil. God's truth sets us free!

Jesus' death at the hands of sinners and his resurrection through the power of God are the ultimate victory over the slavery of sin. We share in that victory when we join ourselves to Jesus and allow his love to change us into truly human persons, not slaves to sin and evil.

Many people think that freedom simply means being able to do anything we want. But that only restricts the freedom of others, and is therefore not freedom at all. For example, if what I want is to have your TV set and I take it, that would deprive you of your freedom to have your TV. Pope John Paul II speaks about this false notion of freedom very powerfully in another encyclical, *Evangelium Vitae* (*The Gospel of Life*):

> This view of freedom leads to a serious distortion of life in society. If the promotion of the self is understood in terms of absolute autonomy, people inevitably reach the point of rejecting one another. Everyone else is considered an enemy from whom one has to defend oneself. Thus society becomes a mass of individuals placed side by side, but without any mutual bonds. Each one wishes to assert himself independently of the other and in fact intends to make his own interests prevail.

Elsewhere in *Evangelium Vitae* the Pope says the following:

> Thus it is clear that the loss of contact with God's wise design is the deepest root of modern man's confusion, both when this loss leads to a freedom without rules and when it leaves man in "fear" of his freedom.

Keeping in contact with God's wise design and exercising true freedom is what our life is about. Learning about this design and this freedom is what this book is all about. I hope you will join me as we explore what is central to our existence as human persons: what does it mean to be a child of God, and how do we live as God's children?

In Part Two we will take a close look at what sin and evil really are and what the Church expects of us with regard to its moral teachings. In Part Three and Part Four we will turn our attention to specific moral issues for which the Church is heavily criticized — teachings on sexuality and life and death. In Part Five we will take up the subject of truth and justice, and in Part Six we will summarize our journey together. In short, we will learn what the Church teaches in specific areas of morality, why it teaches these things, and how we are to use these teachings in our lives. What I hope to give you is a fuller understanding of what it really means to be human, and how the Church helps us to reach our potential as God's precious creations.

All I ask is what the Church asks of you: to have an open mind, a willing heart, and a desire to know both God and yourself intimately.

I think you'll find that you two have a lot in common.

PART TWO:

Sin and Evil

Before we can discuss any of the Church's moral teachings, we need to understand the meanings of two very important words: sin and evil. People often use both of these words to talk about acting against God's ways. They say someone has done something evil, or has sinned. But these words really have different meanings, and cannot always be used one for the other. To understand the role Church teaching plays in our lives, we must first understand what these words really mean.

Evil and sin are both very complicated things which have many different levels and types. I couldn't possibly explore these topics thoroughly here, for to do so would require many books. What I will give you is a very basic distinction which, though relatively simple, should do much to help you understand more about morality and our relationships with God and with other people.

An evil action is anything we do that goes against our nature as people created in the image and likeness of God. Because they are opposed to this image of God, such actions are always wrong. They cheapen us, damage us, prevent us from becoming what God made us to be. They disrupt the natural harmony and happiness which God created. Every evil act we commit contributes to the erosion of the goodness of God's world, and leads to consequences we can't always reverse.

While evil actions are always wrong by their very nature, not all of them are necessarily sins. A sin is an evil action we are directly responsible for and for which we are accountable to God. It is done deliberately, with the intention of either neglecting or directly opposing God. There are circumstances, however, where evil actions aren't necessarily sins. We can do evil without intending to offend God, without realizing it is evil, or because we sincerely don't believe it is wrong in God's eyes. Sometimes we fall into a bad habit which becomes so powerful we really don't have a lot of control of ourselves over our actions.

A sin is doing something we know to be wrong on purpose — not really trying to avoid it. It is possible to do evil and still not sin. Thus all sins are evil, but every evil is not necessarily a sin.

Only God can judge when a person has sinned, for only he can look into our hearts and discover our true motives. God forgives all sins if we are truly sorry for them and show repentance. Yet any sin we are aware of and are not sorry for is liable to God's punishment. We are not held accountable for evil actions which are not sins, but we are responsible for sins we have not sought forgiveness for.

This does not mean, however, that doing evil is right in itself as long as we're not intending to sin. It still disrupts the natural harmony of God's world, whether our intentions are good or not, and so it is wrong in itself. And though we may not be punished for an evil action which is not a sin, doing evil still damages our soul, for it keeps us from reaching the full humanity in which God created us. We may not end up in hell for doing evil which is not a sin, but we may need to be purified in purgatory, because each evil action moves us further from the perfection which is required before we can spend eternity with God in heaven. Being true to our natural goodness brings us that much closer to the perfection which will lead us to our ultimate destiny, which is life forever in joy and peace with God. An example will help explain this, and help demonstrate how even the best intentions do not negate the reality of evil.

A television news show reported the story of a man who helped his elderly father commit suicide. His father was suffering from cancer and wanted to die in order to put an end to his misery. Because the son could not bear to see his father in so much pain, and because he wanted to obey his father's wishes out of love for him, he helped his father commit suicide. The son told the news reporter, "A loving, compassionate God will understand."

This statement about God is correct. God is loving and compassionate, and does understand when people do things like this. The son truly believed he was doing a loving, compassionate, Christian act of mercy, ending his father's pain and bringing him peace. He was also under a great deal of stress, seeing his father suffering and feeling pressured by him to assist with the suicide. For these and other reasons this action may not necessarily have been a sin, for the man sincerely believed he was doing something good in God's sight. As such God probably wouldn't consider this a sin, and if so would not punish him for this action.

But that doesn't mean that what he did was right!

When we perform an act which is basically wrong — such as the taking of a life — all the good intentions, all the difficult circumstances, all of God's mercy and forgiveness can't change the evil of the act itself. Though he had the best intentions and did this lovingly, the son nevertheless committed an act that is wrong, and in doing so helped usher more evil into the world. His action gave into despair, which goes against our nature as people created in the image of a hopeful God. It expressed a lack of trust in God and his plan for human existence, in his ability to heal, strengthen and give comfort to the sick and dying. It showed a lack of respect for life, which God creates and only he has mastery over. It promoted death as a good over life. It cheapened life by claiming that it is valuable only up to a certain point. It robbed his father of the love and companionship which he really needed at this time. Even though we believe that God understood his motives and would most likely not hold this act against him, it was still an act which brought more evil into the world and further contributed to the disruption of God's creation which evil always brings. Even though this man did not consciously do something which he believed was wrong, damage was done to his soul nevertheless. Killing, no matter what the motive, goes against our nature as people created in the image of the God of life. It makes us imperfect and less than human, whether we realize it or not. This man may not be headed for hell for this action, but God will need to purify his soul in purgatory in order to bring it to the perfection which heaven requires. He will still be in relationship with God, but the relationship will need a lot of work to return it to what it was meant to be.

This is the basic difference between evil and sin. They are both wrong things to do, but sin involves a deliberate break in our relationship with God and the punishment it brings if it is not repented in sorrow. We need to understand this difference if we are to have a mature relationship with God. Otherwise we could end up like the rich young man in Matthew's Gospel — following the rules out of a sense of duty but feeling empty because we don't understand the value of following the rules. The value is that the rules are truth, and bring a deep, life-giving relationship with God.

We get a poor sense of morality as children which we hang onto long after it's outlived its usefulness. As a result we can misunderstand as adults what morality really is. As children our sense of right and wrong is centered upon the rewards and punishments of a rule system. Our actions are based on a fear of being punished and a desire to be rewarded.

That's fine for children, because at that simple age it's the only way to effectively teach right and wrong behavior. But as we grow older our lives become more complicated, our minds mature, and childhood answers no longer help. But because these concepts are so deeply ingrained in us, it is often difficult to go beyond them. Morality remains based on a reward/ punishment system from authority, which is really a self-centered system. It looks to what we can get instead of to what we can give to alleviate the needs of others. This can lead not only to a deep sense of emptiness, but to resentment of authority and to rebellion.

As adults we don't make our moral decisions based on whether God is going to punish or reward us. As Christians we trust in the mercy and forgiveness of God, given to us through the suffering and death of Jesus Christ, and in the promise of eternal life to all who believe in Jesus and sincerely live their lives as his disciples.

Our moral decisions are based instead on a deep love for God and for humanity, and a desire to uphold the dignity of every human person. God created the world in perfect harmony. Evil and sin upset this harmony, causing the many troubles we struggle with today: war and violence in all its forms, crime, poverty, materialism, racism, sexism, just to name a few. A mature sense of morality seeks the restoration of harmony in God's world and respect for every human person — regardless of any reward or punishment that may await us. It is based on the good of all creation, not just concern for our own soul.

As people make their moral decisions, they have many different interpretations as to what should be done in order to restore this harmony. Even within the Catholic Church there are many different opinions as to what truly moral behavior is. Catholics are divided over such issues as abortion, artificial birth control, divorce, homosexuality, euthanasia, the death penalty. The Church has specific teachings on all of these issues, but many Catholics disagree with them. Moreover, Catholics who oppose Church teaching often do so in good conscience, sincerely believing they are best serving God by taking the opposite point of view and acting upon it. Just what role, then, do the Church's moral teachings play in our lives?

We've discussed how sin is a matter between an individual person and God, for only they can discern whether or not a person has sinned. So we can't label disobeying Church teaching as automatically a sin, for there are too many factors involved to put it in this category.

But the reality of objective evil is clear. There are certain acts which in and of themselves are evil — upsetting the harmony of creation — whether or not doing them in a particular instance is a sin. The Church's moral teachings serve to define which actions are good and evil in themselves, to help people decide what they should do in particular circumstances.

The Church holds as a basic moral truth that no believer should do something which goes against their conscience, for God did give us the freedom to choose our actions. However, what the Church expects from all of us, and what we are obliged to do as members of the Body of Christ, is to fully inform our consciences about the actions we are thinking of taking. This means learning what the Church has to say about the issue, and then carefully, sincerely and prayerfully trying our best to agree to it. We are called to trust that the Holy Spirit guides the Church and that its moral teachings are true and conformed to the will of God. It is only after we have done all this, and have come to a certain conscience — one without any doubts — that we can responsibly act. Sometimes our certain, fully informed conscience will still lead us to do something that goes against the teaching of the Church. The Church acknowledges this reality, and says that all we can do is obey our certain, fully informed conscience. But we must realize that even when doing an evil act in good conscience, and in good relationship with God, we are still acting in a manner less than fully human and contributing to the disharmony in the world. We are also damaging our souls, which were made to act in accord with the will of God who created us.

There are many people who hold no clearly defined guidelines for what is right and what is wrong. They believe that circumstances always decide what's right and what's wrong to do — nothing is objectively good or evil. The Catholic Church takes a strong, courageous stand to say that certain actions are always wrong, disrupting God's plan for creation, regardless of the circumstances. Whether or not these actions are sins can depend on the circumstances, but the actions in and of themselves are still wrong. Out of its deep love and respect for God and for all of his creation the Church strongly proclaims these truths to the world. It asks that the world listen and seriously consider them, so that the original harmony with which the world was created may be restored.

That's what the Church asks of you, too. It asks you first of all to be secure in your relationship with God through Jesus Christ — to abandon your fears of being punished and your desires for rewards — and to realize that you are loved beyond all imagining. Having accepted that love, the Church then asks that you turn your focus from yourself to God and his creation, loving them with a pure, selfless, mature love. You are then asked to carefully and prayerfully listen to the Church's teachings on moral issues, giving your most honest, sincere and fullest effort to understand them and to try to live by them. Once your conscience has thus been fully formed and is certain of what to do, then do it — trusting in God's love for you and eternal commitment to you. Reflect your commitment to him in your actions.

In the next two sections we will take a careful look at the Church's moral teachings that are most hotly contested today: teachings about sexuality and about life and death.

PART THREE:

Issues of Sexuality

The Church's teachings about sex are well known. Sex should be only between a husband and wife. Couples should not use condoms or any other means of artificial birth control. Masturbation is wrong, as are homosexual acts. People not in a married state should abstain from sex.

The Church is sharply criticized for its stands on sexual morality. Its teachings are called unrealistic, uncaring, discriminatory, irresponsible. As Catholics we are obliged to give these teachings a fair hearing and to genuinely try to assent to them. Let's take a close look at each of these teachings to learn why the Church takes the stand it does.

Sex Only In Marriage

Having sex is the closest you can possibly be to another person. It is a form of communication which says to the other, "I am yours. I give myself to you completely." When sex is entered into outside of a committed relationship it is a lie and something that is ultimately very hurtful to the relationship. When entered into casually, it can give rise later to the suspicion that one's partner may not be faithful. Commitment is very important in a sexual relationship.

But if having sex is the closest you can possibly be to another person, it also makes you the most vulnerable. During sex you literally expose yourself completely to your partner, and share the most intimate, most exciting and most loving of all human experiences. But what happens if you and your partner later break up? You'll be hurting a lot. Nothing hurts more than being loved deeply by another person and then having that relationship come to an end. You feel betrayed, used, and alone. As a result, one of two things will probably happen. Either you will be less trusting of others in the future and will therefore have trouble forming other relationships, or you will immediately look for someone else to have sex with in order to ease the pain caused by your break-up. In either event, your ability to have a truly loving relationship with another person is damaged.

Because being human means being in loving relationships with others, you won't reach your full potential as a human person in a non-committed sexual relationship. This will also affect your ability to have full non-sexual relationships as well. That's why sex outside of a committed relationship is wrong. Not because sex is bad, for by its design it is a life-giving, love-bonding experience. But when it is used casually it damages people and their ability to really love, making them less than what God created them to be. It makes us less human.

So we see why sex outside of a committed relationship is wrong. But why marriage? If two people make a life-long commitment to love each other, can't they just live together without the piece of paper which says they're married?

If marriage were merely a piece of paper, that might be a good suggestion. But marriage is not merely a formality to be put on record. When a man and a woman promise to love each other for the rest of their lives it necessarily involves God, whether they realize it or not, because they are actually participating in God's creative love for the world. Since it involves God it involves marriage, for from the very beginning, God created marriage as his instrument for filling the world with his loving presence. The book of Genesis tells us:

> So God created humankind in his image, in the image of God he created them; male and female he created them. God blessed them, and God said to them, "Be fruitful and multiply...." Therefore a man leaves his father and his mother and clings to his wife, and they become one flesh.
>
> *Genesis 1:27-28; 2:24*

God chose the union of a man and a woman in a committed relationship as the instrument of his creative love for the world. God blesses this union, which means it necessarily involves him. Two people living together does not fulfill this function. The blessing of God in marriage is necessary to uphold the natural dignity of this union. Furthermore, if a couple merely lives together they have made no formal commitment. Therefore there is no real love, for love is nothing without this formal act of total commitment. True love is not afraid to be committed to marriage, so the sexual union will be fulfilling and life-giving — not anxious about whether the relationship will last.

This scripture text further tells us that a husband and wife become one flesh — this finds its fullest expression in the birth of a child. Two people coming together in love literally form one flesh — a baby — a new life born of their love. God's love is life-giving, and so is the love of marriage. This is another reason why a man and a woman joined together necessarily involves God — they're participating in the same creative, life-giving love. It must involve God and his blessing of the union in marriage. Any other arrangement is far below our human dignity as God's people.

Every society from time immemorial has recognized the importance of both parents, not only in the birth of a child but even more importantly in that child's upbringing. A child without two loving parents who are devoted to its well-being is deprived in many ways. It can survive, it's true, and even be successful in life, but there will always be that sense of loss. Real love in marriage is never centered on the couple alone but always looks to the real needs of others, first of whom are their children.

One of the strongest images from the Bible that describes Jesus' love for his Church is that of a marriage; Jesus is described as a groom coming to marry his bride, the Church. Marriage is founded upon that same image. The *Pastoral Constitution on the Church in the Modern World,* one of the most important documents to be issued by the Second Vatican Council, tells us, "Christ the Lord has abundantly blessed this richly complex love, which springs from the divine source of love and is founded on the model of his union with the Church."

That's why the Church teaches that sexual union is reserved only for marriage, and that marriage is the only acceptable state for a man and a woman to live their life together.

Divorce

In the Gospel of Matthew we read the following discussion about divorce:

> Some Pharisees came to (Jesus) and to test him they asked, "Is it lawful for a man to divorce his wife for any cause?" He answered, "Have you not read that the one who made them at the beginning 'made them male and female,' and said, 'For this reason a man shall leave his father and mother and be joined to his wife, and the two shall become one flesh?' So they are

no longer two, but one flesh. Therefore what God has joined together, let
no one separate." They said to him,
"Why then did Moses command us to
give a certificate of dismissal and to
divorce her?" He said to them, "It was
because you were so hard-hearted that
Moses allowed you to divorce your
wives, but from the beginning it was
not so. And I say to you, whoever di-
vorces his wife, except for unchastity,
and marries another commits adul-
tery."   *Matthew 19:3-9*

From our earlier discussion of marriage it
should be clear that this is a very serious,
responsible commitment, not to be entered
into lightly. A marriage involves more than an
agreement between two people. It is an act
through which God himself joins the couple
together to be bearers of his love to each other
and to their children. While two people bring
each other before God to marry each other, it
is God who joins them through their vows.
What God joins together, humans simply don't
have the power or the authority to dissolve.

But problems often occur in a marriage,
and many times the partners reach the point,
for very legitimate reasons, where they can no
longer live together and maintain the relation-

ship. This is a very real problem which happens
to the best of people. The Church understands
the circumstances which can lead to this problem and the pain it brings to all people involved.

The Church also understands the seri-
ousness involved when two human beings attempt to break a bond which God himself
established. Through marriage a couple is no
longer two but one flesh joined together by
God. To tear one flesh in two is painful. God
wants his people to be happy in loving relationships. Divorce breaks these relationships and
causes pain which God does not want. Divorce
is wrong not because people are bad to get
divorced, but because it makes peoples' lives
unhappy, and this is not God's plan for us.

Further, the Church must follow the com-
mands of Jesus, who taught that marriage cannot be dissolved by human beings. It is a permanent bond established by God. As Pope
Paul VI wrote in his encyclical *Humanae Vitae*
(*Of Human Life*):

> The Church, in fact, cannot act differ-
> ently towards men than did the
> Redeemer. She knows their weak-
> nesses, has compassion on the crowd,
> receives sinners; but she cannot re-
> nounce the teaching of the law which

is, in reality, that law proper to a human life restored to its original truth and conducted by the spirit of God.

This is why, when a couple goes to court to get a divorce, the Church doesn't recognize the marriage as over. Though a judge may issue a piece of paper which declares a marriage to be through in the eyes of the state, in the eyes of the Church all true marriages are permanent. (Just as a piece of paper does not make a marriage, it does not break it, either.) That is why the Church will not allow a divorced person to marry again, for the Church declares divorced people to be still actually married.

While the Church will not acknowledge divorce, if the circumstances warrant it, it may grant couples who want to end their relationship an annulment. This is a statement in which the Church declares that a marriage was never valid in the first place, and therefore it wasn't really a marriage. There are a number of conditions which must be met before a marriage can be considered valid. The couple must enter into it freely, without being forced to by people or circumstances. They both must possess the emotional and mental maturity needed to maintain a marriage. They must be open to having children and raising them in the Catholic faith. There must be no other serious reasons why the marriage should not be entered into. If any of these impediments exist, the marriage is not truly a valid one, even though the couple went through a marriage ceremony, lived together as husband and wife, and even had children. If later on the couple can prove that one or more of these impediments existed prior to the wedding, the Church will declare their marriage annulled — meaning it was never really a marriage to begin with. Each person is then free to marry another, since there was no marriage bond at all.

Whatever happens between a husband and wife in a marriage, nothing changes the status of their children in the eyes of God and his Church. Even in cases where marriages are annulled, the Church considers the children of these marriages fully legitimate, and does not hold them responsible for anything their parents might have done. All children come to God on their own merits — as his children and his precious creations.

Artificial Birth Control

Science has invented a number of devices which couples use so they can have sex while preventing the chance of pregnancy. This has become one of the most controversial issues in Catholic morality. Many people will argue that there is nothing wrong with a married couple using artificial birth control — in fact, in many instances it is seen as the responsible thing to do. A couple with a limited income, for example, cannot afford to have a large number of children. It would put a strain on their marriage and on any children they may already have if they cannot have sex without the possibility of pregnancy. There are many other very good reasons why couples feel they should avoid pregnancy and why artificial birth control is seen as the way to go.

In 1968, Pope Paul VI issued an encyclical letter called *Humanae Vitae* (*Of Human Life*). In it he spelled out the Church's position that artificial birth control is in itself a wrong action, for it interferes with God's design for human sexuality. The Pope reiterated the fundamental truth that sex has two functions in marriage: to physically unite the couple in a bond of mutual love and to procreate children. While these may seem obvious, the Pope further pointed out that these two functions are inseparable — couples cannot use sex for one purpose and not for the other. To deny either of these aspects is thus not a full act of love. It is leaving something back, making this an act of incomplete, less than 100% giving. Pope Paul VI wrote:

> … this love is total, that is to say, it is a very personal form of personal friendship, in which husband and wife generously share everything, without undue reservations or selfish calculations. Whoever truly loves his marriage partner loves not only for what he receives, but for the partner's self, rejoicing that he can enrich his partner with the gift of himself.

Any artificial device which prevents the free flow of semen through the vagina is, by its very nature, minimizing the full, free act of love which sexual intercourse is designed by God to be. The pure, human act of intercourse holds no boundaries, just as there are no boundaries to the love between the partners of which intercourse is the fullest expression. In a pure, natural act of sex, the fullest expression of love, the couple gives everything to each other, including the man's sperm and the woman's ovum. Artificial birth control prevents this total giving, making it a limited and conditional sharing between the partners. Any relationship based on conditions and limits rather than total sharing is less than pure human love, and is opening itself up for the problems that naturally come when pure unconditional love is not central to a relationship. If a couple withholds complete sexual union from each other, they can withhold other things as well. This withholding leads to other problems which can eventually lead to the break-up of the relationship. In the United States there is widespread use of artificial birth control. There is also a 50% divorce rate. There could very well be a connection between the withholding of physical love and the withholding of emotional and spiritual love.

Every act of sex between a husband and wife must be both a bond of unity and open to the possibility of conceiving a child. Everything else is far less than what God created sex to be — it is less than fully human.

However, the Church recognizes that there are serious situations in families where the births of children must be spaced apart, or even situations in which pregnancy must be avoided. God knew this too. In fact, God designed a woman's menstrual cycle so that not every act of sex would necessarily lead to pregnancy. Because of these realities the Church does approve of the use of a natural system for the regulation of births called Natural Family Planning. Instead of relying on artificial devices which render the act of sexual love limited and incomplete, this method allows a couple to regulate pregnancy while sharing full, free sexual union the way God intends it to be. Couples keep track of the woman's menstrual cycle, when she is fertile and infertile, and have sex according to this cycle. Couples who practice this method report that it actually strengthens their love and improves their sex life. By abstaining from sex during the most fertile periods they grow emotionally and spiritually closer, focusing on the friendship aspect of their marriage rather than the physical. Without this friendship no marriage can last, no matter how great their sex life is. When they return to sex couples report that it is a richer experience after a brief period of abstinence. In contrast to the general divorce rate, the Couple to Couple League reports a divorce rate of less than 5% among couples who practice Natural Family Planning.

Masturbation

Masturbation is the act of stimulating your own sexual organs and giving yourself pleasure. God designed sex to be both unitive between a man and a woman and procreative, leading to the birth of children. It is meant to connect us to others in a bond of self-giving love. Since masturbation does not have any of these aspects, it is clear why the Church calls this an action that is wrong in itself.

What also makes masturbation a less than human action is that it makes us look to ourselves for fulfillment. When masturbation becomes a habit we can become less interested in relationships with others and more interested in satisfying ourselves. We need loving relationships with others to become full and fulfilled human persons. Masturbation can lead us away from seeking these relationships, and can leave us empty and lonely as a result.

When masturbation becomes a habit we can also become obsessed with sex, thinking about sex more and making it a top priority. This can make us more likely to seek sexual relationships with others for the pleasure it brings rather than as an expression of our love. When this happens we fall into the dangers we've already discussed about casual sex.

Our sexual organs were designed by God to be used with another person as an expression of committed, lifelong love, uniting us to another and creating new life. They were not made primarily for our own personal pleasure. Masturbation leads us to behaviors that are less than fully human, and that is why it is wrong.

Homosexuality

This is another complicated issue in sexual morality, and an area where some fine distinctions must be made. The word "homosexual" has two different meanings when we use it in conversation, and it is very important to understand the difference between these two meanings.

Sometimes we use the word to describe someone with a homosexual "orientation." This simply means someone who feels sexually attracted to members of their own sex, whether or not they are sexually active. Sometimes we use the word to describe someone who is actually involved in a sexual relationship with a member of their own sex. In discussing homosexuality it is important to understand the difference between someone who merely has homosexual feelings and someone who acts on those feelings in a sexual relationship.

There is nothing immoral about having homosexual feelings. That's because our sexual feelings are something over which we have little or no control. Morality is based on decisions we make, and we don't choose our sexual orientation. Some people believe that homosexual orientation is a choice, that homosexuals could be heterosexual if they wanted to be. But the truth which the Church recognizes is that sexual orientation is something we have no control over. Regarding this, the *Catechism of the Catholic Church* says the following:

> The number of men and women who have deep-seated homosexual tendencies is not negligible. They do not choose their homosexual condition; for most of them it is a trial. They must be accepted with respect, compassion, and sensitivity. Every sign of unjust discrimination in their regard should be avoided. These persons are called to fulfill God's will in their lives and, if they are Christians, to unite to the sacrifice of the Lord's Cross the difficulties they may encounter from their condition.

Yet, just as with our other feelings, if we act on them in inappropriate ways we become less than fully human. For example, it is human to feel angry, but less than human to express our anger with violence. In the same way it is human for a person of homosexual orientation to feel attracted to someone of their own sex, but it is less than human to act on these feelings through a homosexual act.

The very nature of sexuality involves the possibility of creating life. Our genital organs by their design are meant for this process — not to be used by themselves, and not to be used with similar ones. The design of the human body is such that the man's penis is meant to go inside the woman's vagina. That's the human act of sex, nothing else.

Celibacy and Sexual Abstinence

So what about people who have a homosexual orientation, or heterosexual people who aren't married? What are they supposed to do about their sexuality — just not have sex? This is a very complicated and important question. Let's look at it in detail.

It's hard to understand Christian sexual morality in today's world, because sex is everywhere. TV shows, movies, commercials, magazines, music, and so much of our modern culture tells us we have to have sex to be a fulfilled human being. By showing so much sexual imagery they arouse us and stir our sex drive so we want it even more. Sex is presented in the entertainment media as being a normal, expected part of any relationship between a man and a woman or a homosexual couple. In movies and TV shows, sex becomes a routine part of dating, not marriage. We get many of our attitudes from TV and movies, and they're always telling us that sex should be as much a part of our daily routine as brushing our teeth or going to the bathroom.

If you're going to look to the entertainment industry as a source for sexual morality, be warned that their record in this area is very poor — Hollywood has never shown a mature, healthy attitude towards sexuality.

For example, in the 1950's and 1960's TV shows were not allowed to show married couples sharing the same bed. Famous TV couples like Ricky and Lucy Ricardo of *I Love Lucy* and Rob and Laura Petrie of *The Dick Van Dyke Show* were always shown in bedroom scenes as sleeping in separate beds. Sex between a husband and wife is the most pure, natural, moral action there could be, yet early TV producers were afraid to show married couples merely talking in the same bed. Why? Because they had an immature and unhealthy outlook on sexuality.

Today on TV it's common to see two virtual strangers having sex, and their relationship is depicted very graphically. Why? Because TV still has an immature and unhealthy outlook on sexuality.

It's best not to look to the entertainment industry for standards of sexual morality. They've never gotten it right.

But it's partly because of the prevalence

of this Hollywood sexual ethic and its impact on our society that people have come to accept that sexual activity should be a part of everyone's lives, and that it is unreasonable and unnatural to expect anyone to abstain. But Hollywood didn't write the script for human existence. You're not a television character made up by some scriptwriter to entertain and to exploit others for money. You're an infinitely valuable human being created by the Author of all life to be a model of his virtuous love through which all of the world was created. As such you have a responsibility — to yourself and to others — to guard your gift of sexuality and to only use it in appropriate ways.

Though we're all "equipped" with sexual organs, not all of us are called to have sexual relationships in our lives. Rather than having that kind of intimate relationship with another human being, some are called instead to have that kind of relationship with God. This includes more than priests and Religious Sisters and Brothers. Many lay people are also called to live a "celibate" lifestyle — giving up marriage and sexual union for the sake of a closer relationship with God and through that with others. As God created sexuality as a love-giving, life-giving gift to be shared only in marriage, anyone not in a married state is expected not to be sexually involved with any-one.

As a celibate myself, I can't lie to you and tell you it's a way of life filled with nothing but lovely and wonderful things. It can be tough. We don't lose our sexual feelings when we decide to live a celibate life, it's still with us. I have the same feelings as anyone else, and it is sometimes very difficult to accept that I have committed myself to a life of not acting on those feelings. Yet sexuality can be shared in other ways which are both love-giving and life-giving, which does not involve any genital activity. So what are some constructive ways to live celibacy in a healthy way?

Let's first take a more in-depth look at sexuality and what it really is.

When people talk about sexuality, they usually refer only to what we do (or don't do) with our genitals. But sexuality is actually much more than that. It includes our total being as a person. Everything we do we do as sexual persons; our sexuality involves every aspect of our lives. We have to expand our understanding of sexuality beyond our genitals in order to understand this. I'll offer you my experience as an example.

I was born a male. Therefore, everything I have ever done in my life, I've done as a male.

I think as a male, I react to situations as a male. I participate in relationships as a male, I study as a male, I minister as a male, I write as a male, I pray as a male, I feel emotions as a male — I live as a male, with a male's outlook and experience.

If I were a female, I would experience all of these things very differently. I'd be in a female body, with a female's outlook, feelings and experience. Men and women have equal status in the eyes of God, but there are genuine differences between the two — physically, emotionally and spiritually. Men and women experience life differently depending on their sex.

That's what we mean by the word sexuality — not just what we do with our genitals, but how we experience our whole lives as either males or females. Our sexuality involves everything we do.

Understanding the true nature of sexuality is the first step in learning to live chastely as a celibate. We all have a sexuality which cannot be denied — to deny our sexuality would be to live incompletely, less humanly. So we have to live our sexuality. But if we think of our sexuality as only what we do with our genitals, then we're bound to channel our sexual energy only through them. Outside of a committed marriage, this will only lead to the problems I discussed earlier. But if we can broaden our understanding and realize that our sexuality encompasses everything in us, we can come to a much better understanding of how to live out our sexuality apart from genital activity. We are then freed to express our sexuality in many different ways.

What, then, are some of the practical ways to live celibately without genital activity? The best way is to develop close, intimate friendships, with people of both sexes. What drives us sexually is a basic need to be connected with other people, to be in union with others. When we can satisfy our need for interpersonal intimacy on the emotional and spiritual level, it makes sexual abstinence much more manageable. When you think about the times you are the most sexually aroused, it is usually the times you're feeling the most lonely, when you're feeling the most emotionally disconnected from others. Our emotions and our sex drive are very closely related, and it's usually when we're feeling lonely that we crave sex the most. What we need are close friendships, where our need for intimacy can be satisfied without having to have sexual intercourse.

Another practical way to express sexuality in a non-genital way is to do something creative. Sex is a creative function, so the more creative things we can find to do, the more outlets we have for sexual energy. Writing is a creative outlet for me. Since I'm celibate and will not procreate children through sexual love, my books become my creations. Any creative talent or interest you may have can be a valuable way to use your sexual energy in a productive, healthy way.

Like any marital relationship, celibacy can be a real burden at times — make no mistake about it. But when it is understood in its fullness and lived in a healthy way it can be deeply rewarding and spiritually fulfilling. Celibacy does not mean abandoning our sexuality, but learning different, creative ways of living as sexual persons. When followed wholeheartedly, these ways can lead to the same kind of fulfillment and satisfaction found in marital love. It can lead to a new level of maturity and spiritual awareness in our relationships with others and with God. And that intimacy can be life-changing and truly renewing.

PART FOUR:

Issues of Life and Death

Whoever attacks human life, in some
way attacks God himself.
Pope John Paul II, *Evangelium Vitae*

Abortion, euthanasia and the death penalty are three of the most bitterly disputed life
issues of our day. In 1995 Pope John Paul II
released what is perhaps the most brilliant
document ever to define the Church's posi-
tions on these matters: *Evangelium Vitae* (*The
Gospel of Life*). I will draw upon the Pope's
insights in discussing the sanctity and dignity
of human life, at whatever stage and in whatever circumstances, and our moral obligation
to defend every human life against all attacks.

All discussion of human life must begin
with this passage from the book of Wisdom:

God did not make death, and he does
not delight in the death of the living.

> For he created all things that they
> might exist… for God created us for
> incorruption, and made us in the im-
> age of his own eternity, but through
> the devil's envy death entered the
> world, and those who belong to his
> company experience it.
> *Wisdom 1:13-14, 2:23-24*

God did not make death — life is God's
only creation. Jesus told the Sadducees (who
did not believe in life after death), "Is not this
the reason you are wrong, that you know nei-
ther the scriptures nor the power of God? …
He is God not of the dead, but of the living; you
are quite wrong" (Mark 12:24, 27).

When God created the human race, death
was not part of the plan. God created human
beings to live forever, because he is the God of
life. Death came into the world as a result of the
devil's envy of our closeness to God and
humanity's cooperation with him. The devil,
the source of all evil, wants people to disobey
God because of his intense jealousy of him. He
uses deception and trickery to get people to
turn from God. That is why evil actions seem so
attractive even though they later cause us misery — it's the devil's attempt to fool us and lead
us away from God. It is because of this relationship between the devil and human beings that

a wedge has been driven into the relationship between God and humanity. The devil led the human race to separate ourselves from God, and the biggest result of this separation is death. Death is the physical sign of the disruption between God who gives life and people who rejected his life. Because people turn away from the God of life, they die. Death is the devil's victory.

But since God is infinitely more powerful than the devil, death is not permanent. The devil's victory is only temporary—the death he caused to come into being is overturned by the everlasting life God gives to all who die believing in him. This is what the death and resurrection of Jesus are all about.

God made the world in perfect order and harmony; humans ruined this harmony by sinning. The result of this disharmony is death. The human race thus had to do something to make amends and to restore the harmony in order to escape death.

But there was a problem. Human beings owed God for disrupting his world, but we're not powerful enough to repay a debt to him. How can a human being pay a debt to God? Only God is capable of paying a debt to himself. But God didn't owe the debt — we did. So how could human beings pay back a debt they owe to God when God is the only one capable of paying the debt — but he doesn't owe it?

The answer was for someone who was both human and God to pay the debt. That's what Jesus did through his crucifixion. When Jesus died on the cross he once and for all reestablished peace between God and the human race. By subjecting himself to the same death which the devil brought into the world Jesus paid all of our debts to God for our sins, past, present and future, and restored forever the peace between God and ourselves. Then he went one better — he rose on the third day, breaking forever death's hold on us and giving eternal life to all who believe in him. While physical death remains because sin remains in the world, it is only a temporary state thanks to the incredible love of God given to us through Jesus.

From this a very strong message emerges: God did not make death, nor does he delight in it! He is God of the living, and all of his actions lead towards life. Even where death occurs, God restores life.

Death is the devil's doing, the direct result of his evil temptations and of humanity's cooperation with him. Only the devil delights in death, for it is the sign of our separation from God.

Thus any attack on human life in any of its stages, under any circumstances, is evil. Attacks on life are carried out in humanity's weakest moments, not our strongest, when we give into the devil's temptations. For in our strongest moments, free of the lure of evil, as people created in the image of a loving, life-giving God, we defend human life in all circumstances.

Yet in all three of the evils we will discuss in this section — abortion, euthanasia and the death penalty — supporters call upon the notion of freedom in advancing their ideas. They will argue that a woman has the freedom to end a pregnancy; that a dying person or their family has the freedom to choose at what time death will occur; that a government has the freedom to execute criminals it considers dangerous to society.

To answer these arguments we must remember Pope John Paul II's teachings about true freedom which we read in Part One. Freedom does not mean doing anything we want — it means being free from the slavery of evil forces which deceive us and tempt us to do things that go against our basic goodness as God's people. When we give into these temptations to do evil, it is the death of freedom, for we become the slaves of evil. Thus we are really not acting freely if we are involved in any of these practices.

Having established these principles of life, let's take a look at each of these three issues.

Abortion

> Can a woman forget her nursing child, or show no compassion for the child of her womb? Even should these forget, yet I will not forget you.
>
> *Isaiah 49:15*

> For it was you who formed my inward parts; you knit me together in my mother's womb. *Psalm 139:13*

In my book *If There Is A God, Why Do I Need Braces?* I wrote the following:

> During the nine months you were in your mother's womb, your mother really had nothing to do with the process of actually building you. She didn't get up in the morning and say, "Let's see, today I'll make the hands, and tomorrow I'll work on the feet. Next week I'll get the nervous system in place, then I'll work on the circulatory system. I'd better get that

digestive tract in place before we go on vacation. The eyes and ears will have to wait until we get home." Nope. Your mother simply waited for you lovingly while you were formed inside of her by some unseen, powerfully creative force.

This idea is expressed in the Bible in the second book of Maccabees:

> I do not know how you came into being in my womb. It was not I who gave you life and breath, nor I who set the elements within each of you.
>
> *2 Maccabees 7:22*

Abortion is the killing of a human life inside the mother's womb, an attack on its dignity and the dignity of its creator. There is no other way to describe it.

The plain truth about human reproduction is that it is a process beyond the control or choice of human beings. God designed and made our bodies, we didn't. Humans have sexual intercourse, but after that matters are really out of our hands. God builds the child in the womb. It is a process over which humans have no active part; we merely stand by and wait for God to finish his work and to receive the new person at birth.

For the human race to interfere with God's life-creating work and destroy it — to assume it's our choice — is perhaps our supreme act of arrogance and our ultimate defiance of God. While other acts of evil and sin can be more subtle, abortion is among the most obvious, for it is the clearest example of humanity rejecting God's plan and death resulting from it.

People have many excuses for justifying abortion, many of which sound loving and compassionate. What about a child whom tests have shown will be born severely handicapped? What about a teenage girl who is pregnant and won't be able to support her child — or is afraid to tell her parents? What about a woman who became pregnant through an extra-marital affair? What about a woman who was the victim of rape or incest? There are any number of difficult circumstances which abortion supporters speak of when trying to justify abortion. They argue that the birth of a child under these kinds of circumstances will only bring suffering.

Yet any suffering in life far outweighs the evil of death. "God did not make death, and he does not delight in the death of the living. For

he created all things that they might exist."
There is no amount of human suffering that
God cannot comfort and heal. A life of suffering is a life — one in which blessings from God
flow freely and the person experiences the love
of God in and through their suffering. Suffering, in fact, brings us closer to God, makes us
trust him more, makes us grow. God does not
come to the world to stop suffering. He comes
to fill the suffering world with his healing
presence. Death cuts off the life through which
God communicates with his people. It is never
an alternative under any circumstances.

We are horrified when we hear of the
murder of an innocent person, such as someone killed by a robber or mugger. Yet many
people who are appalled by that kind of killing
think nothing is wrong with killing the most
innocent and vulnerable of all people — ba-
bies in the womb. As long as we continue to
have this arbitrary attitude towards life, we will
never be free of violence, free of hate, free of
crime and war — we will never be free.

Fr. Frank Pavone, national director of
Priests for Life, sums up the abortion issue very
well: "Love says, 'I sacrifice myself for the good
of the other person.' Abortion is just the opposite: 'I sacrifice the other person for the good

of myself.' Abortion can never be reconciled with truth, love, conscience or God."

Euthanasia

Euthanasia is the killing of a person who is dying or suffering — to ease their pain and bring about death quickly. Like the man who helped kill his father whom we discussed in Part Two, this is always done with the intention of love and compassion.

Regarding this, Pope John Paul II has the following to say in *Evangelium Vitae*:

> Even when not motivated by a selfish refusal to be burdened with the life of someone who is suffering, euthanasia must be called a false mercy, and indeed a disturbing "perversion" of mercy. True "compassion" leads to sharing another's pain; it does not kill the person whose suffering we cannot bear. Moreover, the act of euthanasia appears all the more perverse if it is carried out by those, like relatives, who are supposed to treat a family member with patience and love, or by those, such as doctors, who by virtue of their specific profession are supposed to care for the sick person even

in the most painful terminal stages. …
The request which arises from the
human heart in the supreme confron-
tation with suffering and death,
especially when faced with the temptation to give up in utter desperation,
is above all a request for companionship, sympathy and support in time of
trial. It is a plea for help to keep on
hoping when all human hopes fail.

As we said in Part Two, euthanasia is
giving in to despair, which goes against our
nature as people created in the image of a
hopeful God. It expresses a lack of trust in God
and his plan for human existence, in his ability
to heal, strengthen and give comfort. It shows
a lack of respect for life, which God creates and
only he has mastery over. Since death came
about through the devil's work and was not
created by God, by actively participating in any
death we are cooperating, even though not
consciously, in the work of the devil. Assisted
suicide is a case in point. Euthanasia promotes
death as a good instead of the evil that it is. It
cheapens life by claiming that it is valuable only
up to a certain point. It robs the dying person
of the love and companionship which they
need.

We cannot take God's affairs into our own

hands — we have to wait for him to work in his own time and in his own way. If God did not create death, do we have the right to?

The Death Penalty

Our government has strict laws against murder, clearly stating to our society that killing is wrong. People who are convicted of murder are punished, to further reinforce to them and to all people that it is wrong to kill. Some states, however, have an ironic way of teaching criminals and society that killing is wrong — they kill people who have killed, issuing the death penalty. They tell a convicted murderer that their action was wrong by committing that same action against the murderer. Furthermore, they do this in an attempt to stop violence in the world.

Violence has to come to an end somewhere, otherwise it won't end at all. When the state promotes and practices the killing of criminals it only teaches that killing is alright after all. It fosters an attitude of violence in all members of society, continuing to erode respect for life. All life is precious to God — whether that of an innocent child in a womb or the most vicious killer in prison. God does not delight in any death.

Issues of Life and Death

Some people defend the death penalty in the name of Christianity — they say that God is in favor of it. But the Bible clearly shows that God does not favor this kind of punishment. In the book of Genesis Cain kills his brother Abel. God punishes Cain but He does not seek his death.

> Cain said to the Lord, "I shall be a fugitive and a wanderer on the earth, and anyone who meets me may kill me." Then the Lord said to him, "Not so! Whoever kills Cain will suffer a seven-fold vengeance." And the Lord put a mark on Cain, so that no one who came upon him would kill him.
>
> *Genesis 4:13-15*

In the Gospel of Matthew Jesus says, "Love your enemies, and pray for those who persecute you, so that you may be children of your Father in heaven; for he makes his sun rise on the evil and the good, and sends rain on the righteous and on the unrighteous." (Matthew 5:44-45) In a parable Jesus compares evil people to weeds planted by an enemy in a farmer's garden of wheat.

> The slaves said to him, "Then do you want us to go and gather them?" But

he replied, "No, for in gathering the weeds you would uproot the wheat along with them. Let both of them grow together until the harvest.
Matthew 13:28-30

Some people will argue, "When a person takes someone else's life, they lose the right to their own." According to whom? Certainly not God. Think about it — if God believed a person loses their right to live when they take another's life, then he himself would take a killer's life after they have killed. Murderers would die on the spot if God demanded their lives in exchange for the lives they take. But God allows killers to continue to live. If even God allows this, what gives us the right to do any differently? Like abortion, the death penalty is a supreme act of arrogance and the ultimate act of defiance against God, for it is premeditated killing in which people assume the right to decide who shall live and who shall die.

Not even a murderer loses his personal dignity, and God himself pledges to guarantee this. And it is precisely here that the paradoxical mystery of the merciful justice of God is shown forth.
Pope John Paul II, *Evangelium Vitae*

God, who preferred the correction rather than the death of a sinner, did not desire that a homicide be punished by the exaction of another act of homicide.

St. Ambrose, *De Cain et Abel*

Do not repay anyone evil for evil, but take thought for what is noble in the sight of all. If it is possible, so far as it depends on you, live peaceably with all. Beloved, never avenge yourselves, but leave room for the wrath of God; for it is written, "Vengeance is mine, I will repay, says the Lord."… Do not be overcome by evil, but overcome evil with good.   *Romans 12:17-19, 21*

PART FIVE

Issues of Truth and Justice

There is no shortage of dishonesty and injustice in our world. There is also no doubt that these evils leave nothing but trouble in their wake. We know about politicians who lie to get into office, about companies who sell cheap products to make a profit with no concern for the needs of the consumer, or who pay their workers poor wages in order to save money. We know about people who cheat on their taxes, take things without paying for them, tell lies to try to stay out of trouble or to get what they want. We know about people who do these things and get away with them, either because they have never been caught or the justice system has failed to bring about fair punishment.

Yet dishonesty and injustice are more than universal problems which affect our world as a whole — they are realities which you and

I have to face in our individual lives as well. In this section we will look at the importance of both honesty and justice in our lives, and how a Christian views each of these important virtues.

Dishonesty is by definition a rejection of the truth. The truth is that human beings are created in the image and likeness of God, and are called to live in that likeness. Thus any form of dishonesty is a refusal to recognize our true nature and likeness to God. As we've discussed earlier, the further we move from that likeness, the more empty our lives become. Honesty — with ourselves and with others — is the only way to reach our full potential as human persons and thus to be truly fulfilled.

Injustice occurs when the truth is rejected and people are treated as if they are not the image and likeness of God; when people are oppressed and treated without dignity. Thus truth and justice go hand in hand. We cannot have a fully human life without either of them, and we cannot have one without the other.

One of the reasons honesty is so hard is that it forces us to recognize that we are not living up to our true nature as children of God. When we take an honest look at ourselves we realize that we have sinned, that we have not been what we are supposed to be, that there are things we have done which bring embarrassment and shame. Why do these things make us embarrassed? Because we realize that they go against our nature. We know by instinct that we are supposed to be good, because each of us naturally bears the image of God inside of us. So the very reason why we find it so hard to be honest with ourselves is that deep in our hearts we know that we are made in God's image, and that many things we do go against that image. Our honesty reveals that we have not been true to ourselves, and it is the shame caused by the truth that keeps us from seeking it.

As a result we can stop growing in our spiritual life. We know we are called to be holy, but we realize how far we have strayed from that goal. We think that to be holy means to be always good and saintly, and when we realize we are not that way we can despair and even decide to give up. Honesty with ourselves sometimes makes us think that we are not capable of being holy at all, and so we avoid both honesty and holiness altogether.

If we think of holiness as being always good and saintly, we are bound to give into despair. The forces of evil and sin are so strong in our world that we give into them pretty easily, and we see holiness as an unrealistic goal. So instead of thinking of holiness as always doing the right thing and being good, let's look at it another way. Let's look at holiness instead as realizing the true relationship between God and ourselves, and the proper role each one plays in the relationship.

The first thing we have to realize is that God understands that we can't always live up to our true nature by ourselves. If human beings were capable of being good by themselves, Jesus would never have had to become human and die on the cross. God had to become human to help us out — he knows we can't do it alone. So the first step to true holiness is to be honest with ourselves and admit that we sin and do evil things, and that we can't do good by our own efforts alone. We can't honestly say "I'm holy" unless we can also honestly say "I sin."

The next step to holiness is then asking God to fill up what is missing in our lives. We can't invite God into our lives unless we acknowledge that there are empty places for him to fill. If we say that we have no room in our lives for weakness, no room for improvement and growth, then what we are really saying is that there is no room in our lives for God. God can only work in our lives when we admit that there is room for him to work, that there are weaknesses for him to strengthen, empty places for him to fill, sins for him to forgive. In other words, God can only work in our lives when we are honest enough to admit that we need him. So holiness is really recognizing the relationship between God and ourselves, and recognizing the proper role of each of us.

Thus we can't really have a relationship with God unless we are first honest with ourselves and recognize how much we really need him. But our relationship with God is not just a private matter. We need to be in relationship with the other people God put in our lives in order to be in full relationship with him. The same honesty we need with God is also required with others if we are to have truly fulfilled relationships with all of them. Once again, this can be difficult, because honesty with others also involves admitting doing things we may not be proud of. It is even harder to admit these to others than it is to admit them to ourselves. But realize that this embarrassment has a positive side — it means we're aware of our true nature and we really have a desire to live by it. We wouldn't be embarrassed about the wrong things we do if we didn't realize how much we are called to be like God, and if we truly didn't want to live up to that calling. If we didn't recognize and want our relationship with God we wouldn't care about the wrong things we do. By our very nature we desire a relationship with God, and we hurt when we realize that it has been broken in any way. The only way to restore the relationship is to be honest enough to admit when we have done wrong and express our sorrow for it rather than make excuses for it. Making excuses for our wrong actions is a denial of the truth, and gives us a life based on falsity. This will eventually lead to more long-term pain than will the temporary embarrassment of admitting our mistakes.

As long as we continue to live in a world where the pull of evil is so strong, we will continue to be drawn into it and do wrong things. The way to deal with that reality is not to deny it by covering up our mistakes and making excuses. We deal with our mistakes by accepting responsibility for the times when we do fall, being sorry for them, confessing them in the Sacrament of Reconciliation, and moving ahead with an honest self-knowledge and honest relationships with God and with others. God understands that we sin — there is no need to hide from that reality. Learning to be secure in our relationship with him will help us attain that honesty.

Whenever a lie is told, no matter how big or how small, more evil is admitted into the world. The truth of God's goodness is further eroded, and his people suffer more. Some of the effects of dishonesty are quite dramatic, and we'll take a look now at some of these.

One of the biggest effects of the rejection of truth is injustice — when things aren't fair. Examples of injustice abound in our world. Some people have more money than they know what to do with while others go hungry and homeless. Innocent people suffer from a variety of afflictions — war, crime, oppressive governments, sexual exploitation, and many other assaults to human dignity. All of these have as their root cause the rejection of the truth of human nature, accepting instead a false notion that not all people are created equal in the image of God. As long as we continue to treat any member of society as being less than human, our society will remain less than human, less than what God intends, and thus far below what we can be. A concern for truth and justice should be in the hearts of all Christians, and we should do what we can to promote them in our own lives.

Two parables from Jesus will shed light on our discussion on truth and justice — what they really are and why they have become so distorted in our world. The first one goes like this:

The kingdom of heaven is like a land-owner who went out early in the morning to hire laborers for his vine-yard. After agreeing with the laborers for the usual daily wage, he sent them into his vineyard. When he went out about nine o'clock, he saw others standing idle in the marketplace; and he said to them, "You also go into the vineyard, and I will pay you whatever is right." So they went. When he went out again about noon and about three o'clock, he did the same. And about five o'clock he went out and found others standing around; and he said to them, "Why are you standing here idle all day?" They said to him, "Be-cause no one has hired us." He said to them, "You also go into the vineyard." When evening came, the owner of the vineyard said to his manager, "Call the laborers and give them their pay, be-ginning with the last and then going to the first. When those hired about five o'clock came, each of them re-ceived the usual daily wage. Now when the first came, they thought they would receive more; but each of them also received the usual daily wage. And when they received it, they grumbled against the landowner, say-ing, "These last worked only one hour, and you have made them equal to us who have borne the burden of the day and the scorching heat." But he replied to one of them, "Friend, I am doing you no wrong; did you not agree with me for the usual daily wage? Take what belongs to you and go; I choose to give to this last the same as I give to you. Am I not allowed to do what I choose with what belongs to me? Or are you envious because I am generous?"   *Matthew 20:1-15*

This parable has two important things to teach us about truth and justice. First, all people are equal in the eyes of God, whether others recognize it or not. When God gives himself in love he has to give himself completely, for God is total, unlimited love. For God to give more to one person and less to another would go against his nature as a totally giving God. As we said in Part Three, love is total, unlimited and unconditional. God loves all his people the same, no matter how much more one may have done for him than another. Furthermore, we can't earn God's love by what we do — it's given to us for free, and it is given to us in full. All of us are entitled to God's love. The workers hired first in the story thought an injustice had been done because those who worked only an hour got the same pay as them. This is the world's view of justice. But to be jealous that God loves another as much as he loves us even though they have not done as much as we have is really an injustice in the eyes of God. So our first lesson from this parable is that we need to be concerned that all of our neighbors receive the fullness of God's love, and not to be looking to recieve more of it than others.

Second, this parable shows the relationship between honesty and justice. The first workers to be hired were promised a certain wage, and they promised to accept it. At the end of the day they wanted more than what they agreed to. Their desire for more is based not on their original promise, but on what they have seen the others getting. The workers have broken their promise of the wage they would accept, while the owner has been faithful to his promise. Whenever we are unfaithful to a promise we are being dishonest, and injustice results. So our second lesson from this parable is that we need to be true to our promises no matter what others are doing. Honesty does not depend on the actions of others — it is true in itself, and cannot be changed.

Our second parable goes like this:

The kingdom of heaven may be compared to a king who wished to settle accounts with his slaves. When he began the reckoning, one who owed him ten thousand talents (one talent was worth more than fifteen years' wages!) was brought to him; and, as he could not pay, his lord ordered him to be sold, together with his wife and children and all of his possessions, and payment to be made. So the slave fell on his knees before him, saying, "Have patience with me, and I will pay you everything." And out of pity for him, the lord of that slave released him and forgave him the debt. But that same slave, as he went out, came upon one of his fellow slaves who owed him a hundred denarii (a hundred days wages — a much smaller debt than what the first slave had owed); and seizing him by the throat, he said, "Pay what you owe." Then his fellow slave fell down and pleaded with him, "Have patience with me, and I will pay you." But he refused; then he went and threw him into prison until he would pay the debt. When his fellow slaves saw what had happened, they were greatly distressed, and they went and reported to their lord all that had taken place. Then his lord summoned him and said to him, "You wicked slave! I for-

gave you all that debt because you
pleaded with me. Should you not have
had mercy on your fellow slave, as I
had mercy on you?" And in anger his
lord handed him over to be tortured
until he would pay his entire debt. So
my heavenly Father will also do to every one of you, if you do not forgive
your brother or sister from your heart.
Matthew 18:23-35

In this parable the first slave owes a huge
debt — more than fifteen years wages. Tradi-
tional justice demands that he pay back what
he owes, but he doesn't have enough money.
Even if he sold everything he had, the slave
would still never be able to repay the debt.
Justice cannot be truly served in this situation,
because the resources to do so just aren't
there. If justice cannot be done, another plan
must be put into action to resolve the situation.
When justice is so far out of reach, the only
answer is mercy. The king forgives this impossible debt rather than demand the impossible
payment. Mercy replaces justice in this situation, and at this point in the story all is well and
order is restored.

This is exactly what God has done with us
through the death and resurrection of Jesus.
The human race, through its sinful ways, ran

up such a huge debt to God for spoiling his world that there was no way we could repay it. He cancelled the debt through the blood of Jesus on the cross. When Jesus was crucified, the justice of God was transformed into mercy and forgiveness, and this in turn became the order to be followed in the world.

But mercy can only work as a means of restoring order if it in turn is given and multiplied. Yet the slave does not do this. When he meets a fellow slave who owes him a much smaller, more payable debt, he will not extend the same forgiveness which resolved his case. He returns to the old order of justice, and in doing so his world falls apart. The king revokes his mercy and reinstates justice for the slave, for this is the measure which the slave chose to use.

In the same way the mercy which God extends to all of us can only restore order on earth if we in turn extend it to others. Through Jesus Christ the justice of God has been transformed into mercy, and this becomes the new measure by which to solve the imbalances in our world. True justice can only come about through true mercy.

As we reflect on this in our own lives, we need to ask ourselves: Do I seek justice or mercy in my relationships? When someone

GOD COULD BE A TEEN

wrongs me am I more concerned that they "get what's coming to them" or am I more concerned that they feel the healing power of mercy and love which can soften their hearts and enrich their lives? God will treat us in the manner in which we treat others. If we forgive, God will forgive us. If we demand payment from others, God will demand payment from us. This is only fair, and so, by definition, this is justice. How we want to be treated by God should be the measure of how we treat others. Only in this way will true justice ultimately prevail.

Honesty with ourselves and others, even when it hurts, brings us to God. Honesty in all of our activities — schoolwork, jobs, sports — brings about justice. Respecting ourselves and others as people created in God's image and likeness brings about peace. Pope Paul VI said that if we want peace, we must work for justice. The justice we need is that of God, which is merciful, instead of that of the world, which is vengeful. True peace and God's justice go hand in hand.

> Peace I leave with you; my peace I give to you. I do not give to you as the world gives. Do not let your hearts be troubled, and do not let them be afraid. *John 14:27*

PART SIX:

The Point of It All

> If I have told you about earthly things
> and you do not believe, how can you
> believe if I tell you about heavenly
> things?   *John 3:12*

Jesus speaks these words to Nicodemus as
he struggles to figure out his faith. The Church,
the body of Christ on earth, speaks the same
words to us as we face the same struggle. If we
don't believe the Church's teachings about the
earthly matters of our day to day lives, how can
we believe its teachings about heavenly things?
How can we believe that the Church contains
the full means of salvation yet choose to ignore
certain teachings which are basic to our relationship with God?

As Catholics, and furthermore as human
beings created by God in his image and likeness, we have an obligation to God who made
us and sustains our life every day. Further-

more, we have an obligation to listen to Church teaching in a spirit of docility — willing to be taught by it. We owe our attention and openness to God's will as revealed to us through the teaching of the Church. Only by such sincere, prayerful attention can we truly live our vocation as faithful followers of God.

Realistically, not all Catholics can abide by certain teachings in conscience. The Church teaches that Catholics are obliged to follow their consciences in areas of morality, and should not do anything which goes against their conscience. However, along with this obligation comes the obligation to fully inform our conscience — to listen to Church teaching openly, to honestly try to assent to it and understand it, and to prayerfully try to place it in our hearts and act upon it. It is only after we have done all of these things that we can then act on our conscience. Our conscience is only of real service to God, to ourselves and to others if we nourish it properly. Just as you wouldn't run a marathon without first training and nourishing your body, moral decisions should not be made without a proper preparation of conscience. Only then are we truly free to make decisions, free of the bonds of ignorance and prejudice which lead us to make poor decisions.

I hope the presentation of moral issues in this book will be of help to you as you face the particular issues and questions in your life. You can count on the stability and soundness of the teachings I have presented, for they are not my own — they are the wisdom of a 2000 year plus tradition, formed by God, instituted through Jesus Christ and guided by the Holy Spirit. You can trust it, rely on it, believe in it.

When you get discouraged by the great amount of evil and sin in the world, realize what has brought it all about — the rejection of these truths. We have in our Catholic tradition the truth that can change the world, if only the world would accept it and live by it. Keep living in the truth, share it with others, defend it and love it — and the truth will continue to live. It will continue to make a difference in the world, to be a light in the darkness of sin, to be hope in a world of despair, to be life in a culture of death.

The truth will keep you on the path of life. The truth will set you free.

> All who commit themselves to following Christ are given the fullness of life: the divine image is restored, renewed and brought to perfection in them. God's plan for human beings is this,

that they should be "conformed to the image of his Son" (Romans 8:29). Only thus, in the splendor of this image, can man be freed from the slavery of idolatry, rebuild lost fellowship and rediscover his true identity... The purpose of the Gospel, in fact, is "to transform humanity from within and to make it new." Like the yeast which leavens the whole measure of dough (cf. Mt 13:33), the Gospel is meant to permeate all cultures and give them life from within, so that they may express the full truth about the human person and about human life.

Pope John Paul II, *Evangelium Vitae*

Works Cited

Catechism of the Catholic Church. (Washington, DC: United States Catholic Conference, 1994).

Merton, Thomas. *Conjectures of a Guilty Bystander.* (Garden City, NY: Doubleday, 1966).

Pavone, Frank J. "New Abortion Rhetoric: God and Conscience" in *Priests for Life,* January, 1996.

Penrice, James. *If There Is a God, Why Do I Need Braces?* (New York: Alba House, 1995).

Pope John Paul II. *Evangelium Vitae,* 1995.

Veritatis Splendor, 1993.

Pope Paul VI. *Humanae Vitae,* 1968.